The Spaces Between Birds

Wesleyan Poetry

Sandra McPherson

The Spaces Between Birds

ᴇ *Mother/Daughter Poems*

1967–1995

Wesleyan University Press

Published by University Press of New England / Hanover and London

Wesleyan University Press
Published by University Press of New England, Hanover, NH 03755
© 1996 by Sandra McPherson
All rights reserved
Printed in the United States of America   5   4   3   2   1
CIP *data appear at the end of the book*

The following poems are reprinted by permission of The Ecco Press:
   From *Elegies for the Hot Season* © 1970–1982 by Sandra McPherson:
"Pregnancy," "Labor," "Pisces Child," and "On the Move."
   From *The Year of Our Birth* © 1978 by Sandra McPherson: "Children."
   From *Patron Happiness* © 1979–1983: "Games," "For Elizabeth Bishop,"
"Preparing the Will, Three Generations," and "Lifesaving."
   From *Streamers* © 1988 by Sandra McPherson: "Lament, with Flesh and
Blood," "Flowering Plum," "Conception," "Maureen Morris, Mother of
Five, Eats a Pansy from the Garden of a Fancy Restaurant in Aspen," and
"Note to Sappho."

❧ *for Phoebe*

Contents

Preface

Twenty-eight years of poems keep each other company here. I was a determined but anxious mother: I wrote poems to help me think. My daughter's own poems and youthful statements participate, too. The result is in no way a full chronology of such an intricate person; it is, however, a fairly complete selection of responses, to important steps in mothering, that reached the level of art. We both grow up over the span of the decades of poems. I am proud of who my daughter is. She is much more than these poems can catch.

Because the poems were composed over many years and in differing life contexts, pronouns may represent different people from poem to poem. Close reading should clarify identities. The sequence also reflects divergent diagnoses, from poetic and eccentric to hyperactive to learning-disabled to schizotypal to Asperger's syndrome autistic. Some of the poems were published under a pseudonym; others never saw publication; a few appeared in print but remained uncollected.

I am grateful to Dr. Oliver Sacks, and to Gwen Head, Joan Swift, Pattiann Rogers, Minnie Bruce Pratt, and Susan Kelly-DeWitt, mothers and poets, for encouraging me to assemble this collection. This book is my "hug machine."

S. M.

The Spaces Between Birds

From the Horoscope Cast in Seattle
Following My Daughter's Birth

PHOEBE BORN FEB. 24, 1967, has her Sun in Pisces with Neptune as ruler of the sign. It is related to arts, especially music. It has affinity with love for the helpless and exploited and perhaps most animals. Pisceans make good spies and detectives.

When Phoebe was born, one planet, Mercury, was especially significant. The planet was in retrograde motion. This symbolizes a mind inwardly turned either because of a mystical trend or because of a congenital slowness of perception and an inability to project thoughts outward. Mercury in her chart will be in retrograde motion until she is 23 years old, when it changes to direct motion. At this period there will be a change in her thinking and she will be more outgoing in her thoughts.

Outwardly, Mercury may give a slow mind but by no means necessarily so. It may just as well be a mind preoccupied mostly with the collective unconscious, the mind of a seer. We say that "there is more there than meets the eye." It creates a sort of backward condition but allows the person to try again and again.

She is personal about impersonal issues, and impersonal about personal issues.

First word: "Machine!" —age 1 ½ or 2

"To be or not to be: that is not a question." —age 4

"I'm a pretty historical girl." —age 5

ONE

Child

Pregnancy

It is the best thing.
I should always like to be pregnant,

Tummy thickening like a yogurt,
Unbelievable flower.

A queen is always pregnant with her country.
Sheba of questions

Or briny siren
At her difficult passage,

One is the mountain that moves
Toward the earliest gods.

Who started this?
An axis, a quake, a perimeter,

I have no decisions to master
That could change my frame

Or honor.
Immaculate. Or if it was not, perfect.

Pregnant, I'm highly explosive—
You can feel it, long before

Your seed will run back to hug you—
Squaring and cubing

Into reckless bones, bouncing odd ways
Like a football.

The heart sloshes through the microphone
Like falls in a box canyon.

The queen's only a figurehead.
Nine months pulled by nine

Planets, the moon slooping
Through its amnion sea,

Trapped, stone-mad . . . and three
Beings' lives gel in my womb.

Labor

"You'll forget about it,"
I didn't want to,

Pupil in the white of an eye,
Only thing that could see.

The starving of Leningrad
Shrank back and forth on the pavement

Three stories down; in her Demerol
Pond the fish slowed.

Awake! awake! awake!
And when I'm not it's babble

Or a rabbit nose,
Everyone's normal case.

My belly's an old hill in childhood.
To think of the texture

Of anything else—an oak leaf,
Sand—it's impossible.

Little bullet,
Come out, come out!

I've a slim dress to wear,
I've a joy.

Pisces Child

Those calm swamp-green eyes,
Gliding like alligators,
Float to this shore
And bump awake.

Sea-legs jerk.
Hands swim still, submarine pink, the palms
Stretched out like starfish.
I'm the old wharf you live on.

Your tongue draws oceans in, not spitting
A word out. Quick, fluttery, slight
As a guppy,
Coercive as undertow.

Oh paramecium
I am your gross-pored mama. Hydra,
An elephant
Suckles you.

In the wilderness you are a spring.
You perpetually melt,
Lake and river maker, dedicated as the porpoise
To return to the sea.

Do you want both worlds?
I see you rooting,
Arms random, then possessive, like potatoes
Sprouting.

Or, needing, needing to need,
You cry yourself purple as eggplant.

You are wordless, but never mind:
You have your sort of song.

It can be heard above the breakers.
I watch you, you're far out on the horizon.
I am landlocked as a cat.
You will never run dry.

Poem for My Child, with a Line by Seferis

Seeing you naked
twining up his arm,
your buttocks walnuts
in green rinds,

the pouch of your torso
an oriole's nest,
your knees
pinto beans

as simple as
your undressed feet
sound—

*So much nakedness
is almost blood.*
It is almost I.

Such tight clothes
could only have been sewn
by bones.

Such bones
could not but let
the raw muscles
love them, twining.

Mother and Child

Thinking of Henry Moore

1

Today clouds churning like whales threaten
Our bare heads. Across the plaza, city hall
Squats against a concrete cake of steps.
Daffodils rip down an edge of the park walk.
You and I are pieces of some inheritance, a jewel box,
Pearl, flounce, in the male city,
Before these square public buildings of heavy stone.

2

We haven't a rocking chair and yet
Something jars the delicate air continually.
It seems our nature, child, to stir
And alter everything as a bird peck-pecks
Day into its shell and the gnats
Make mad circles in the forest air. And why?
Over my knees, my shoulders, you climb,
Testing the stability of this non-rocking chair.

3

The river bow, the bud, the limpet, the fig—
These are the forms we grow from.
The dome, the cup, the bomb, the bomb—
These they wrest from us, certain sculptors
Of woman in the straight-lined world.
Sitting for the camera, we slip, double,
Sympathetic and worn, among our places for each other,
Worn round, and "sitting" the way the world spins.

On the Move

Town to country to town again we're on the move.
Your shirts are packed like a kill of ducks, my fox
Hat bristles at its cage. For a month
We're strong as coolies paid the wages of our possessions.

To look at painful as a sunburn this wallpaper
Must peel. The porch sags,
Lap sat on too long. In the basement a black
Widow fights for your hand and squatter's rights.

We're the new government. The patria we rent.
Your suits fly loyally in and out of the door.
We keep a wilderness in adytum,
Den, scriptorium. The walls we tax with paintings.

Cat-eyed, the baby whets
Her nails on the plaster. She'll tame—
In time to move out, move on, packing these bodies
We home in and hers, the tiny, only house we've built.

⚘ *[Early Language]*

"I hear pineapple" [vibraphone]
"I hear noodles" [yodeling]
"Purse-papa" [mailman]
"Temperature broom" [electric fan]
"Red in the body" [stomach ache]
"Nutritional love."

My face looks like jellyfish
My forehead looks like lights in the sky
My forehead looks like snails
My eyes look like stars
My nose looks like buttons
My mouth looks like poison fangs
My body looks like snakes
Snakes are nice
My intestines look like squirrels
My hair looks like eggs
My teeth look like bugs
My shoulders look like doors
My cheeks look like elephants
My elbow looks like bears
My legs look like alligators
My ears are perfectly
My ears are lightly
My body is perfectly

[Asked "Are you a little girl or a little boy?"]
   "I'm a little man."
[I repeat the question]
   "There's a little ox crying."

Butterflies by a Lake

I am told she speaks strangely
And should seek help.
To the psychologist I bring
This mud lit with butterflies:
She said this . . . and this . . .
Orange sayings, midway
From blood to the sun,
One opening then another,
Elegant echolalia —
And the softness of her speech,
Confusing pronouns, so that
You and *I* are changed:
CHRYSALIS: we cannot be told
Apart; and he can tell us —
What? — to speak for oneself,
Little and veering in the sun.

Eschatology

I accompany this life's events like a personal journalist:
"Little did she know when she got in the car that after-
    noon . . .";
or "Despite inauspicious beginnings,
this was to be their happiest year."

Little did I expect that our horoscopes would prove true.
And how could we foresee an answer to
that frankly secular prayer, we with so little faith
as to be false prophets to our most fortunate gifts.

I am glad when doom fails. Inept apocalypse
is a specialty of the times: the suffering of the rich
at the hand of riches; the second and third comings of wars.

Shouldn't we refuse prediction
that the untried today is guilty, that immeasurable
as this child's hope is, it will break tomorrow?

"This place is full of dogs and full of dumb meaning."

Mamas talk civilized
talk like chipmunks
bears

I like to hug you
to skunk you
to learn the numbers with you
yeah!

Are you a dry mama are you?
Is it wet inside your skin?

Children

She will run to you for love whoever
you are, you who'd forgotten what you look like.
She keeps a book of forms in her arms,
like a fitter exact on waists.

And perhaps I'll have to pull her from
celebrating her birth between your legs
although she is my only child
and good at it and best of all the children

you don't have. You know her face
can't be yours. But let me become a stranger,
not act myself, beat on the mirror and cry —
she sees I look like her alone.

And sticking her face in mine, smearing my
lipstick with her index finger, igniting
the pale mustache, drawing the seeing mirror
of her glasses down oil

on my cheeks, she hangs my picture
forever in her head. So that she always
sees to me when I am down
and thinks the way to raise me is

to climb aboard me toe for toe, palm
lidding palm so I can't withdraw
or go out of our single mind
to have another child.

Lament, with Flesh and Blood

I do not know much about innocence
but it seems you are responsible
for this evening lake's young blue that laments
how fishermen joke and loons laugh. Sibyl
of leeches, you're young but you're scary,
dangling your thin, taut, clarifying legs
at fish cleanings in the estuary.
Fog stars the knives that slip out pike eggs.
Blue's future is black. The present is rain.
The past is rain the wind blows back.
Still you sit—Audubon, catch that blue vein!—
a tiny funnel bisecting your cheek.
I want you to run to me with your kiss.
Still you brood in the lake like wild rice.

Games

I play pool. I aim toward the faces
    Across the room. My daughter
Takes these quarters for the pinball
    She plays with a dying

Butterfly on her left hand. It
    Will not leave, it is tired,
And all its strength is in its legs.
    I set it on my arm

Then give it back. I'll take her hand
    That way when dying, stick
Out my tongue, like its curled black one,
    Green crutch of a Kentucky

Wonder Bean, and *Look,* she cries,
    Its body fell away.
It's all wings and head. Short life
    Has culled mistaken

Parts and dropped the mite-sized heart and
    Killed the steering place.
Or else she did this, quickened its
    Death among the games

And flunked it too soon. And even so
    The golden-mica'd wings
Are best. She forgets it easily,
    Who never speaks of losing.

For Elizabeth Bishop

The child I left your class to have
Later had a habit of sleeping
With her arms around a globe
She'd unscrewed, dropped, and dented.
I always felt she *could* possess it,
The pink countries and the mauve
And the ocean which got to keep its blue.
Coming from the Southern Hemisphere to teach,
Which you had never had to do, you took
A bare-walled room, alone, its northern
Windowscapes as gray as walls.
To decorate, you'd only brought a black madonna.
I thought you must have skipped summer that year,
Southern winter, southern spring, then north
For winter over again. Still, it pleased you
To take credit for introducing us,
And later to bring our daughter a small flipbook
Of partners dancing, and a ring
With a secret whistle. —All are
Broken now like her globe, but she remembers
Them as I recall the black madonna
Facing you across the room so that
In a way you had the dark fertile life
You were always giving gifts to.
Your smaller admirer off to school,
I take the globe and roll it away: where
On it now is someone like you?

They've bought the world
They put some soap on it
So it won't rust
And they put new mamas in it and new houses in it and new
    families in it
They bought the world so they could put new plants in it,
    new fertilizer
They put new streetlamps in it
So the world won't be empty
They put new toys in it—they were made of wood—
And new schools
The giant salesman bought the world
They put the world in a clown's body
And they put the clown in a joker's body

Preparing the Will, Three Generations

She fills each little link
    Of the gold chains
We are asked to choose among
    With her tears;
She fears inheritance,
    The turning to shadow
Of fingers filling the opal rings
    We could select.

Oh don't be afraid,
    I say, Heaven
Is even more made of these things;
    That's where your
Grandparents are going; heaven
    Is even more
Lapis lazuli like these
    Piercing anemones
For Grandmother's ears.

Then those tears, too, appraised:
    She thinks she is
Too sinful and cannot
    Join them there.
Best ask for the ladderback chair,
    Or that glass sparrow
God's eye would glance
    Clear through:

Nothing directly changing hands,
    No sapphire watch,
Blue as the vein
    Under my mother's

Cirrus-thin wrist,
    For a hellion. Best ask
For the iron and board—
    And maybe the loudest radio—
Like they have in hell.

Easter 1979

I remember the crucifixion
that April, the neighbors frozen around it,
those with—on their bumpers—"I Found It."
There would be no resurrection

of the limp brown monkey
my daughter nailed through stuffed wrists
so that its neck muscles languished,
the passioned head fell forward, a lanky

rhesus, evolutionary Jesus.
It draped beside my sign to keep the garbage men
from trampling Gethsemane,
our heartland vegetable garden.

Never less simian in their hats and gloves,
homing churchgoers couldn't tell
blasphemous evil from the mentally ill,
and passing up a scarecrow puffed with bur-oak leaves

reviled the mind that looped a tail
around a hickory-twig cross's central spar,
indicted my girl
so poised so young in arts of sacrifice.

Christ, your abstinence
denied us neighbors more divine,
dilute descendants of the Truth and Life.
We too could have been in your bloodline.

But as it is, when boat-tailed grackles
pray in their unoiled call

on both sides of your effigy,
my only beloved daughter feels

not fright but artistry, not thieves but wings.
And she stands to the side and cackles.

Lifesaving

You and I are like an old married couple
Since I pulled you from the swimming pool
(The "blueberry pie" you once described it)

In the evening sunshine of Dunsmuir, California.
My parents, that old married couple, stretched just beyond
    seeing
On the motel lawn chairs. They were wearing
Fresh clothes and smelled of shower soap.

They watched the rotating colored light play
Through the fountain and over the petunias
(Which must have thought it weird,

In their simple mind). The dust was settling
Out of the air from the highway project.
We had been going south all day and tomorrow
We would go south.

And they never found out. Your father
Never found out. Only in my mind
Do I hear your close call.

We dried off, it was a perfect evening,
The motel owner was playing "The Blue Danube" on his
    piano.
Mt. Shasta changed in the sunset like the petunias.
You looked over at some teenagers kissing in a shadow;

And you said, "So that's what love is."

🐦 The Old Valentine

It has a ship with hearts on the sail
It has a little red flower
And they have two doves talking to each other
They're talking about the lawn
    about the springtime when the flowers grow in the lawn
    the kids play on swings and slides and merry-go-rounds
The doves are talking about the summer when people go to
    the beach
The doves are pointing their beaks together
because they want to talk about the different plants in the
    world,
    different kinds of flowers
and there's a whole valentine filled with roses
and it has these blue flowers—
how about a blue clover?—
I know what to call this flower:
I'm going to call it a white night rose
The flowers sleep at night
They dream about lots and lots of camellias
Here's some more red flowers—camellias
Here's a blue ribbon tied around the stems
and here is a golden wall
And this valentine has three wooden hinges to keep it open
They move like our arms
This has a golden ship
It's floating along in red water
because the flowers are reflecting in the water

TWO

Woman

Flowering Plum

On the sole half-day she can be alone
    she learns that there are plum-recluses,
or were, all year waiting for transparent
snowy nights in China to begin spring.
In the flowerless back of the exhibition hall
    she lies across a bench. February
in the south; people in new cloth shoes.

    Her daughter, able now to be home alone,
    leans shirtless in an open window,
        a hermit of exhibitionism.
    Her double new ignited breasts,
    fervescent as melting ice,
    are womanly enough to bend
        a branch, to twist a mind.

It is work to gladden your one mad girl.
    When you need to travel
she fears all scenery but herself.
You book passage down the necks of flowers;
her turned mind balks as if *in utero*
    until you feel the blossom
force again, the doubling begin.

    In moonlight which brings the woman home
    her child throws a radio out the window.
        A tantrum through the thin-ply air, mist
    threaded between stars. The blossom vases
    shudder with the stamping of her feet.
    The woman hears breakage—
        of petals, the radio caught by a tree.

Drunk, one recluse munched the blossoms
  for a midnight snack.
He made them travel down himself.
Drunk, a woman pinned some blossoms in her hair,
in the morning found damp calyxes,
    another year's seclusion.
Drunk, plums' first cold-venturing bees.

A child hangs washed jeans to tighten
on her mother's branches,
    moss-patched, rough and twisted,
broken at their furthest, weakest reach.
On the whorl where stresses flow.
Flowering, flowing plum, winter petals:
    We are a single mother, an only child.

Conception

I was seeing, as the police
came again this week, that moment
of pleasure in your student room—
carefully darkened with serious
bindings and a pulldown lamp
that left, to patrol beside our love,
only a glowing woolen peony.
Others' facsimiles of our heat that year
initiated embryos that today have pressed
our daughter against the bridge rail
and thrown her schoolbooks off to educate
commuters' tires, truckers' windshields.
Her Spanish doe's eyes now
are black with fear and hate.
                              In those days
we were translating a Spanish poem
almost gory with *rosas*, one we
finally hid from English because it had
too many *corazón*s. Into that world
we brought a child. Into our house
old pleasures have brought police.
And as one picks the softest chair
to bundle his hip revolver in,
I remember you were thinner then.
I counted your ribs.
You were starving, nearly, surviving
on corned bear-meat
which you tweezed with chopsticks.
I was fat. You sighted along my thigh
for one last moment when
there would be just two of us.

. . . And we sit now in the wooden chairs,
pinning as much hope on the officer's badge
as on a star in the blue.

Bad Mother Blues

When you were arrested, child, and I had to take your pocket-
knife
When you were booked and I had to confiscate your pocket-
knife
It had blood on it from where you'd tried to take your life

It was the night before Thanksgiving, all the family coming
over
The night before Thanksgiving, all the family coming over
We had to hide your porno magazine and put your handcuffs
undercover

Each naked man looked at you, said, Baby who do you think
you are
Each man looked straight down on you, like a waiting as-
tronomer's star
Solely, disgustedly, each wagged his luster

I've decided to throw horror down the well and wish on it
Decided I'll throw horror down the well and wish on it
And up from the water will shine my sweet girl in her baby
bonnet

A thief will blind you with his flashlight
                                    but a daughter be your bouquet
A thief will blind you with his flashlight
                                    but a daughter be your bouquet
When the thief's your daughter you turn your eyes the other
way

I'm going into the sunflower field where all of them are facing
me

I'm going into the sunflower field so all of them are facing me
Going to go behind the sunflowers, feel all the sun that I can't
   see

‮ *The A,B,C,D, and F*

The A is the note you tune up on.
The A is one of the best grades.
The B is the crisp note.
The B is the "O.K." grade.
The C is the "in between" grade.
The C is the note you put the piano bench right in front of.
The D is the "almost flunking grade."
The D is the note that sounds old fashioned.
The F is the melancholy note.
The F is the flunking grade.

Maureen Morris, Mother of Five, Eats a Pansy from the Garden of a Fancy Restaurant in Aspen

I don't know what she'd been saying about her life.
At lunch we all shared—
pasts, minor points of minor histories—but oh
if we hadn't been chosen to live them. . . .
My detail told about a child
reeling, first time drunk, swimming
to her parents' ankles, reaching out
like a mystic gripping roots
to make it down
a steep trail to the river.

Maureen pictured us deserving better—
Carol, Ava, Lolly, the mothers—
deserving to choose what we give birth to.
And why, even, does it have to be human?
Why not that nodding purple avens in Hallam's marsh,
eyelid flower turning to feathers?
Why not a green bog orchid
more after our own kind?

And so we are waiting: It is not too late
to give birth to a flower,
never an irreconcilable seed.

Maureen heads between full tables
to a free purple face wholly open,
adopts it with a snap and eats,
passes it around our table,
does this in noon light, one bite
for each child we conceived in the dark.

Note to Sappho

In an age when T-shirts are our libraries,
doing laundry is a literate job.

My daughter puts a clean one on
and her seventeen-year body is an open book.

But when she takes it off, on just another
virgin night, she says Mom it's hard

to sleep against my breasts. Agreed,
but I don't curse them. Sometimes I curse

the mattress springs, get up and read
you under the lamp. Or clear-imaged lines

of my former teacher, lesbian,
you would like. Otherwise, no birds

will sing for two more hours yet.
I hand-do the indecipherable lingerie—

cups that would strain wine!
Then lie down and dream your life

linked in bumpy sleep with mine.

Some Schizophrenics

1
The dearest made good poets.
One used to declare
all poems were about her;
another, that she liked
insects in clothes—
pants, suspenders, dresses, shoes,
nice colors.
She didn't mean fashion.
She was old wool, out-of-fashion.
Both were polite,
poor as pigeons.
One night
one's mother threw her
out of the mansion.

2
Early morning fish-light.
One month married,
I walked by a coyote
on my way to cross a river.
Foetus-high. Moss-slick cobbles.
The father on the other side.
I carried a mind like that
in my hips.
I did not know
it would fit nowhere else.

3
My heiress sleeps, she is
a woman, she sleeps

the whole time
flowers are alert.
I tire of waiting.
I sleep. She stirs,
gets dressed, and bikes
the empty night streets.
Her ankles trail fog.
I sleep and cannot know this.
It's not half spring,
mold-season for oranges,
smoky coals,
silvery lambs
lost within the sheepfold.

4
Learning the wisdom
of deep space from television,
I write astrophysics
on an orange
and place it on her pillow:
"Each thing is the center
of the universe."
Each thing—the center.
Place it right
where she can cosset it.
A second orange, blank.
Two a day,
eat two a night.
There is no other center.

5
Already a woman,
she will rise,
as I flannel and soap

myself for bed,
and stalk me until she hugs
her centers
into mine
in wrestling, longwinded embrace:
Shall we breakfast together?
And why not? The moon's
just risen.

6
Today
she goes to bed
as I pick up
the morning paper.

It scares a flicker.

Fog falls
from yellow catkins, fog
in divisions of cones,
roots beaded in it.

Or a morning of dew
washes the webs
heavy and square
as napkins, dew
down low and laundering.

Or the sun comes out.
A jay shadow moves
in the lemon tree.
Green lemons, black motion
playing in the leaves,
the thorns.

No bird is in the tree.
I'm watching
black motion playing
where the whole bird should be.

Of Birds and Their Metaphors

Now that she is nineteen,
her best metaphors are squandered.
But once she said, "You're brushing your hair
like a dead bird."

How I moved that brush
and its sparrow or thrush
through my believing intuition,
sure she spoke true

of songs ripped from tangles,
true of the shine of death.
Fifteen years later my angel of simile
musters only "Capitalist pig!"

Maybe it's from metamorphosis I ache. I beg
rebirth as the lovelier figure.
I redden from the back-
slap of those porcine bristles.

For I wanted to be
her impossible thing
of shampoo and thrushes, of elegy
and mountain quail whistle.

There are lots of "Let's see's" in my mouth.
"Let's see" is like a bird that keeps flying into my mouth
when I'm talking.
My name will just fly away and say Pheee-bee, Pheee-bee.

Measurings, Work and Worth

Between 1968 and 1972 I kept a journal, a written time clock, of how many segments of minutes and hours I worked as a housewife. I wrote poems and needed to spend the time on them that art demands. So I compensated myself, on the journal's time-card, $4.50 an hour when a magazine paid to print a poem. Once I earned $3 for the first printing of a poem; republished, the poem earned $500 more. That created a problem—it cancelled out too many hours of housework. But before the reprint, that poem taking a year to write brought in $3 and gave me forty or so minutes free to write another poem.

*

Working out the rules necessary to this project had its difficulties. When the cat killed a shrew and I cleaned up the violence, or even held a burial, I could write down the time. Floors; cooking. But reading fairytales to my daughter was less simple. I took pleasure in the green, orange, and black illustrations, in the texture of the old cloth cover, the life of the worn threads interpretable as warp holding together my own childhood. My adult mind wandered back on each image. I would forget to check the closing gesture of the minute hand as the story ended.

Count sewing? I loved to cut, to seam. Count blackberry picking? But count washing off the baby feces smeared on a hundred toys—her own hideous art project—while I worked oblivious, in an upper room, on a poem.

But not the cleansing of the dirty knife cutting the poem, dirty with the poem. Do not count that.

*

Like this one, half knife, half poem, set unnaturally in the past tense, and never finished so never, of course, paid for to count against my hours:

> I could not be scary when I screamed.
> I undressed and cleaned
> The barn floor of the baby's room
> On my knees.
>
> Yet I longed, those days, to play
> With the grasshopper, the worm,
> The shrew, the spotted slug,
> Heaven's little gag
>
> For the easily offended.
> Skull and bones of my own making:
> I purified everything of hers.
> Scrubbing, I remembered
>
> Red alder rain falling, patting,
> The willow swishing,
> While her feet had brushed
> Inside me.
>
> What we call "human,"
> When we say we recover it,
> Is the warmth toward each other
> Expressed by animals . . .

*

Years later, packing in the attic to move, I found the document. No minutes ever rounded off, nor dollars, nor cents. Pages and pages, different pens, thick, fine, colors. Columns of times. A great poet should know the time in which she lives; I learned that from reading Auden, a great man of two continents. He learned the time zones.

But I clocked myself going from room to room.

Harmonies for the Alienation of My Daughter

I wish I could put her in the birdhouse.
Evicted from her rented room,
she pushes a wheelchair through rain
when only prowl cars can watch her.
I am tossing, it is no dream
she pushes her belongings through night rain
to someplace wet and cold she will belong.
How have I let this happen?
I wish I could put her in the birdhouse.

Some days she bikes to work,
washes the unmovable man in bed,
cleans the quadriplegic quarterback's
cave and then his parrot's cage,
fastens baby's breath in the paralyzed
woman's hair for the opera.
Some days she comes home fired, lies
down in earphones on the floor,
and cannot cry.

If she is moth-crazy (nice Navaho for mad),
she makes reparations to the moths
by opening the night door to her light.
Then she goes up on the roof,
says it is covered with little white rocks
and mushrooms. Says: "It is so silent."
Says: "The stars are writing a bit
like you but not keeping a file on me
like you." Says: "Mother—

Mother's crazy too."

Images

The town was small to the feet, small around one's body.
The young woman, our acquaintance, had shaved her head
unexpectedly—she sat bald in the most popular restaurant.
My child said hello, memorized the image. Didn't
look long. She was not embarrassed by the change.
This was the first time she had seen such a thing.

My girl *was* ashamed of my silly theatrical wig.
For no reason she could see, I was playing with an image
that should have been mere costume, limited
to masquerade, to drama, or strictly to backstage.
I should not be lunching in the most popular restaurant
in the small town with her, my likeness.

The hair was not from my own body, it wasn't from anyone's.
Leaning away, she wouldn't look me in the eye.
But very little embarrasses my daughter now
except looking pretty. Seeming womanly.
Her hair is cropped like stalwart seaweed on a rock.
It means she wants to have a workable image, a look of work.

She doesn't mind looking different:
She rides a wheelchair around the city streets—
almost all her friends use wheelchairs.
Once, she stepped out of hers, picked me up off the ground,
in a hug, the way an athlete in practice will wrestle
a skidding dummy. Yes, she can walk.

No one around us noticed. "They must be artists," she said.
To them, it seemed perhaps representative of her,
that two-sided image, first piloting the wheelchair,
spinning the steering rims, then lifting, looking proud,

carrying me about on foot. Both actions made physical,
made compulsory, by the texture and propulsion

of an image within herself, by intimacy with others'
marvels of heads and bodies, to whom she gave,
in effect, residence within herself.

*I was trying to make this house shiny with laughter on the
    leaf.*

℞   *Poem about the Evenings*

*When I am walking in the twilight of the evening I feel like a
    bird
flying home from a hard swim at the pond in the sun.*

The Spaces Between Birds

Sick of parental art—"poets have messy houses"—
my daughter assembled an utterly

clean craft, taking all her
favorite vocals and splicing

the scores of pauses singers need
to draw in air for the next phrase,

editing these on a mudslide of a tape
without an electron

of melody until

each outcry had been hushed
to accent

the continuous _____ she wished to save,
a trail of corroboration:

"I breathe, therefore it's in me to sing again."
And it sounds like

    huh
    ah
    hhh
    www
    - - -
    _ _ _ _ _
    ^ ^ ^
    ¡ !

So many things the gasps were not—
not geisha fan flirtations, not uvulations like the gills of fish,

not rings of breathing as in yoga.

They were huffier,
and the sound was an opera

of surmised last words,
Brahms' frustrated false teeth falling—

a sigh and a growl, expulsion
of wisdom

from a sublime
life in music to the secrecies

of rests. Perhaps she could do

the same with hawks or owls.
Or, for grandeur, as a final symphonic movement,

the last few living lions between roars.
And none of her own _____ was on the tape.

One only hears ragged inspiration
welcomed in

and in
and in,

everybody gasping in strong wind,
with no release.

I believe

if we all agreed
to follow each other

in a migratory V,
almost as if because we shaped it with our wings it could be

pronounced in the sky,
we would learn to hear the blankness

that forms the essence of our going on,
some puff we didn't

mean to say but which
means *us*.

"I believe in God,"
she says, censoring

all fallible lyrics of anyone's beliefs.

One Way She Spoke to Me

I would say, "Whisper." And she could
never figure how to do it. I would say,
"Speak louder," into the phone, nor
could she raise her voice.

But then I found such a whisper, the trail
as she began to write to me in snails,
in silver memos on the front door,
in witnesses to her sense of touch.

Home late, I found them slurred
and searching, erasing the welcome
she'd arranged them in:
H—twelve snails. I—seven or six.

They were misspelling it,
digressing in wayward caravans and pileups,
mobile and rolling but with little perspective,
their eyestalks smooth as nylons on tiny legs.

I raised her in isolation. But it is these snails
who keep climbing the walls. For them, maybe
every vertical makes an unending tree—
and every ascension's lovely.

Why else don't they wend homeward to ground?
But what do *we* do? We are only a part
of a letter in a word. And we are on our
bellies with speech, wondering, wondering slowly,

how to move toward one another.

Every single thing except the core of the earth gets touched
  by something.
Every little tiny detail, parts inside toys, parts inside ma-
  chines.
Only the core of earth has never been touched by man
and never will be.

My heart is the core of myself.
When you get an operation or see yourself through an x-ray,
you see the core of yourself,
the heart that makes you live.

Beware of heart attack, the personal core destroyer, the
  death-giver
and finest armed weapon.
Life is the best thing you could possibly have.
For if you had something you liked best,
what would be the good of it if you weren't alive?

If you operate to the heart, your tools will not melt.

Precious Metal

> " . . . though I spoke with the words of 'the world,'
> my gestures were the more important language
> of 'my world.' . . . Fascination for colored and
> shiny objects. Grasping the concept of beauty in
> simplicity. Also a tool for self-hypnosis, needed to
> help calm down and relax. Often closeness to
> particular people lives within these objects whether
> or not they were actually given by the other person.
> A particular color of blue . . . , a bright golden
> yellow button . . . , a piece of cut glass . . ."
> (Donna Williams, *Nobody Nowhere*)

On edges of door keys:
Tetons and fish flashings
    if you look at them;
perfect teeth, balky snarl
    if you use a new one.

She's the apparatus they all fit, a finder,
fascinated with fasteners,
    with shiny messengers
tripped from bicycles,
    charismatic mechanisms.

Each thing seems happy with
its sprung identity—flattered
    that for her to choose it
it must be obdurate alloy,
    no soft supple foil.

It's her brilliance
she's collecting:
    "I have two big jars of nuts and bolts.
My latest find, on the Interstate,
    an offset irregular screwdriver,

can get into a tight area.
You know what I've been using for center punches? —
        spindle from an electric fan;
the center pin of a solenoid;
        a mainshaft from a car—

it's splined at one end.
Old CB antennas make good little fetchers.
        Dental tools:
they're good pulling up a wire."
        Such gear must first

fall out of the sky, be kicked or thrown
or sprained apart. All must be left
        to be alone, missed,
even berthed for good in the ground.
        And the smell of metal—

always, to me, a disappointment,
like can-poisoned pineapple—
        is essence enough to her,
inspiring its body. Each cool instrument,
        attaching to others,

builds a mind across weather.
A bridge, a broadcast tower.
        She doesn't feel the same
about found money:
        It's nice but

it's not a real appliance,
not as personal as one.
        You can't break it for use.
She has the mushroom-hunter's gift,
        to be driving the speed limit

and spot a fraction of some device.
Eyeglasses' screws
          emit seeable light
at a distance. In my slow and easy walks
          I uncover the same

dead crow wing for months, or a swift
whipping lizard tail under thistles,
          and leave each there
to be naturally of use. Or I'll imagine
          a silver pine cone

with no reason to be.
Chrome rainwater in ditches is never,
          to me, a stretching tool.
But an old seer—in his radio repair shop—
          she met when she was twelve

showed her how to mend
and not to break. A good way to change
          your life, she says,
(and it's quicker, more certain
          than regeneration

for lizards or anything botanical)
is learning how to solder metal.
          With each gadget
she translates into being,
          my floral wisdom loses a petal.

Then, with new and mystic
trust in welding, gains it back.

Acknowledgments

Poems from *The God of Indeterminacy* (University of Illinois Press, 1993) are reprinted with permission of the University of Illinois press.

I am grateful to the following magazines for their original printings of these uncollected works: "Mother and Child" in *Concerning Poetry* © 1973; "Butterflies by a Lake" under a pseudonym in *Jam To-Day* © 1978; "Of Birds and Their Metaphors" in *The Threepenny Review* © 1987; "Some Schizophrenics" in *The Missouri Review* © 1988; "Measurings, Work and Worth" in *The American Voice* © 1994; "The Spaces Between Birds," "Precious Metal," and "Images" in *Field* © 1995.

Some of my daughter's poems appeared first in the following publications: *"But Is It Poetry?" — An Anthology of One Line Poems,* edited by Duane Ackerson, *The Dragonfly* © 1972; *The Dragonfly* 13 © 1973; and *Miracle Finger,* edited by Dick Bakken and Charlene Lowry, Salted Feathers © 1975.

The epigraph to "Precious Metal" is taken from Donna Williams's *Nobody Nowhere: The Extraordinary Autobiography of an Autistic,* © 1992 by Donna Williams, published by Times Books, and is reprinted by permission of Random House, Inc., New York.